7 Easy Ways to Make $1000 - $10000 A Month

Easy Step-Step Ways for Anybody

to Start Making Money Online

Copyright Information:

Note from the Author

The purpose of this book is to show you how to make money online in 7 easy steps. Just like me, I suspect most people will stick with this long enough to make a full-time income, but making passive income of an extra few hundred dollars a month isn't too bad either. Throughout this book I'll equip you with the right tools to increase your money making potential.

I am a very to-the-point type of person and I prefer meat to fluff. So, rather than filling this book with unnecessary links and information, I'm keeping it crisp and concise to help new and intermediate online marketers. The steps I give you truly anybody can put to work and make money online and I'll even show you how to sell pictures online, yes that's right, take pictures and selling them online. Depending on how hard you want to work you could make a little or a lot of money every month.

If you're already acquainted to the online world, even a bit, you will realize that there are a lot of people who are making it big in the online world. They are making continuous flow of passive income. Let's get started !

Contents

Introduction

In the early 2007, I was talking to a friend of mine about sharing my ideas to help people. After brainstorming a bit, we decided on a couple of topics I was passionate about: Entrepreneurship and Financial Freedom.

My first idea was to write a post on Financial Freedom each day and comment on it. As I explained this to my friend, he told me that I need a blog. I didn't know what a blog was but I thought, "Ahh...OK, sure."

So for the next few weeks, I gathered as much information as I could about blogging and ultimately decided to create a blog about Financial Freedom. I'm very interested in helping people in becoming financially free, so blogging seemed to be a great way to reach people from all over the world.

Over the next couple of months, I started writing regular blog posts on entrepreneurship and financial freedom. At this point, I thought of making money from my site but had no idea how and honestly, I didn't think it was possible to make a living from it. I put Adsense up on my blog and got my first seven cents!

From there, I tried new methods to monetize my blog. I'd set a goal to make $100 every month by the end of 2007, which was fairly easy.

I should also mention that from 2007 to 2008, I spent less than four hours simply writing articles and the money followed.

By end of 2009, I was earning more than $500 per month.

I'm still a bit in awe as I write this but I can't believe I'm actually paying my bills and expenses from my blog. Rather, I'm learning new ways each day to monetize my blog to increase my passive income. The best part – I'm making money by doing something I'm really passionate about.

Over time, I have discovered more ways to earn money and I have used my experience to write this book. Regardless of what your goals are keep on reading. I'll try to keep everything concise in just 7 steps so that you can start earning money today!

Step 1: Start your niche website

Affiliate marketing is not just ideal for blogs, but for websites too. You can actually incorporate it into small niche sites, authority sites, and personal brands. Small niche sites usually consist of four to ten pages and are dedicated to a specific product. If you want to make money from a small niche website, you should take note of the following:

- Finding a niche and popular keywords that do not have much competition and then building a website that target these keywords do not work anymore. You need to realize that the competition over keywords is tough. Also, Google introduced changes in algorithm that prevent spam websites from showing up in the search results.

- Instead of targeting a specific niche, you should target a specific product in that niche to make it easier for you to create content. If you are able to do this, your site will have a better ranking on the major search engines, particularly Google. Niche sites that have spam-like content are being filtered out.

- Affiliate marketing is basically referral marketing. It works by word of mouth. You can successfully recommend a certain product or service to people who trust your credibility.

How to Choose a Niche

A niche is basically a topic that serves as the main focus of your site. For you to find the right niche, consider the following:

What are your interests?

Create a list of the subjects that you are interested in. Write down your professional and personal interests. Think of the things that you enjoy.

For instance, if you are into photography, you can share photos, tips, and videos about photography. Your target audience would be people who are also interested in photography, amateur photographers, and photography students.

Next, you should think of the things that you would want to learn more about. For instance, if you have always wanted to learn how to cook, you can write about food or recipes. You can discuss various ingredients or discuss the pros and cons of organic food choices.

Finally, you should think of the things that you are currently into. For instance, if you have recently gone back to school, you can write about universities, online degree programs, and tips on how to balance studying and working. Your target audience could be people who are into higher education.

Are there other people who are also interested in your interests?

Baking, modeling, and sports are some of the most popular topics. These niches are guaranteed to have an audience. But what if your chosen niche is quite unusual? How can you know if there are other people who may also be interested in your niche?

Well, you can use Google AdWords Keyword Planner. It is a keyword research tool that is available for free. It will let you search for keywords that are related to your niche, as well as let you know the search volume of such keywords.

You can also use UberSuggest. Whenever people look for something through Google, the top sites that are most relevant to their keywords appear on the search results. You can type in your niche keyword to see the suggestions that will pop up.

You can also use Amazon to search for books about your chosen niche. Check out how many books are available, and read their reviews.

Doing so will allow you to know what people usually search for on Amazon.

Furthermore, you can view discussions online about your chosen niche. Visit forums and Q&A networks, so you can know if there are people who may appreciate your content. You may even promote your site in these places.

Can you monetize your niche?

If your primary goal is to earn money, you have to ensure that you can monetize your niche. Basically, if your niche is related to things that can be purchased, then you can monetize it.

For instance, people who are into photography are likely to purchase books about photography and cameras. People who are into baking are likely to purchase baking supplies and cookbooks. They are also likely to enroll in baking classes.

If anything can be purchased in relation to your niche, you can find an affiliate program that offers items related to it. Amazon is a great suggestion because it has an affiliate program and it sells a variety of items.

If you want to earn money from ads, you can try BuySellAds. It is an ideal marketplace for researching websites that are related to your niche. You can also try affiliate networks such as the programs mentioned in a previous chapter.

Narrow the field.

The final step is narrowing down your niches. It is easy to be overwhelmed by different niches, but at the end of the day, you are better off with just one niche. Focusing on a single niche will allow you to develop a solid launch strategy and improve it with every subsequent launch.

Step 2: Break Limits through Blogging

Think of a blog as an online journal, a virtual notebook if you will, where you can write about anything and everything your heart desires. But the only difference is that your online blog has the potential of being seen and read by millions and millions of people, as oppose to your physical blog/journal/diary which is usually kept in your nightstand where only you and the occasional nosey family member has access to.

The fact that a blog is live and accessible by anyone and everyone who's online paves the way for a plethora of money making opportunities. Here are a few ways you can make money from blogging. ·

- **AdSense**. It's one of the easiest ways to earn money online. Advertisers pay Google to place text ads and image ads on several blogging platforms. When these ads are placed on your site and visitors click on them, Google in turn pays you. It's as simple as that. There are also other alternatives to AdSense that operate in the same manner but with slight differences.

    o MSN adCenter

    o Chitika

    o Reachli

    o Qadabra

    o PPC (Pay Per Click) ads

    o CPM (Cost Per Thousand) impressions

- **Affiliate Programs**. Another great way to make money with your blog is by signing up with affiliate programs. These are networks that let you advertise other eBooks and information products created by other people. In doing so you would receive a commission or fee for every sale that was transacted through your blog. Be sure to choose a product that would be beneficial and informative to other people. The more value the product possesses the higher the chances visitors on your site will be inclined to purchase it. Some popular affiliate programs or networks are:

- o Click Bank

- o Amazon Associates

- o Commission Junction

- o Clicksor

- o Google Affiliate Network

- o HostGator

- o Max Bounty

- o Link Share

- o Apple Affiliates

- o AWeber

- **Private Ads/Sponsorships**. Once your blog starts to rake in some pretty serious traffic, you'll be able to sell or rent banner space to various advertisers who'd like to advertise on your site. This method of making money is really only effective if you have a high traffic blog, otherwise no one would be interested in advertising on your blog. Some individuals choose to charge a onetime fee while other may charge a month rate to rent the ad space. Depending on your traffic and search engine rankings, you can charge anywhere from a few dollars for an ad space to as much as a few hundred dollars.

- **Write Sponsored Reviews**. Many companies are willing to pay bloggers to write honest reviews about the products that they sell and the services they provide. Sometimes they'll even send you the product for free just so you can try it out. When writing the reviews you're often required to insert a link to either the company's website or a page highlighting the specific product. Here are a few sites that provide bloggers hundreds of advertisers willing and ready to pay you for your blog review.

  o Link Post

  o Sponsored Reviews

  o Review Me

  o PayPerPost

  o Social Sparks

  o Bloggerwave

  o Blogsvertise

  o Blog to Profit

  o In Blog Ads

Start Making Money with Blogs

Before you dive into this opportunity head first, here are a few things you should keep in mind as to make your blogging transition and overall experience an enjoyable and successful one.

1) Write about topics you're passionate about. Let your blog be about things you're interested in. This will help your daily blogging and writing flow better, ideas and new topics will come to you easier, and you'll be more excited and motivated to keep up your blog for the long run. Many blogs fail and don't last but a few weeks or days even because they simply possess no value to the blogger.

2) Always offer value to your readers and visitors. This could be in the form of news updates, how-to's, informative topics, coupons and discounts on products and services, or pure entertainment. The more value you provide to people, the more they will be interested in future offers which can result in monetary compensations.

3) From your theme to your colors, borders, fonts, and logos; everything on your blog should mesh seamlessly together. The more cohesive your blog appears, the more appealing it'll be for visitors. People don't realize that the aesthetics of a blog can be just as important as the content.

4) You never want to over commercialize your blog with ads here and there, offers jumping out from every angle, and a pop up for subscriptions every few minutes. This can be a huge turn off to visitors. Your blog will literally scream "I WANT TO MAKE MONEY!" which in turn can have quite the opposite effect.

5) Always use reliable services when it comes to dealing with sales transactions and receiving payments from customers. One of the most widely used electronic payment service would be PayPal, but there are other great alternatives available. Here are a few you might want to look into:

· Google Checkout

· Amazon WebPay

· Dwolla

· Square

· Paydivvy

· WePay

Tips to Get Started Now!

Fortunately, blogging doesn't require a degree or some kind of certification. Anyone can blog; men and women, young and old, professionals, students, even your grandma can blog if she wanted to. And while there are no prerequisites to blogging it does help if you have a little knowledge of grammar and can formulate readable sentences. So if you're ready to jump into the blogsphere, then here are 5 simple steps to start blogging.

1) First and foremost, you have to decide on where you want to create and host your blog. While there are many great blogging platforms available two of the most popular ones would have to be Blogger and WordPress.

· Blogger is owned by Google and is really easy to use and maintain. It has many traffic management tools available to its users and it can cost you as little as $10 a year for a custom domain name or you can opt for the free BlogSpot domain name, e.g. yourblog.blogspot.com

· WordPress is a more sophisticated and highly customizable blogging platform. There are many awesome tools, plug-ins and themes available on WordPress that will help you personalize and promote your blog. You can purchase a custom domain for $18, map an existing domain to WordPress for $13, or choose the free domain that would then appear like this:

yourblog.wordpress.com

If you'd like to see what other options you have available to you then check out the following blogging services and platforms.

· Tumblr is a free and lightweight blogging platform that makes linking and sharing easy.

· Technorati is a real-time search engine for blogs that track the most current and popular blog postings.

· Posterous is another free platform that allows you to create blogs in an email format.

· Blog.com is a fully featured, powerful publishing platform that's free and offers you several awesome features.

· MyBlogLog is a social network for both bloggers and blog readers who want to connect and share insights with bloggers.

2) Next thing you want to do is to go ahead and open up an account with your desired blogging platform. Fortunately, many of these blog services have tutorials and step by step guides that show you how to get everything set up. For the purpose of this demonstration, we'll go over how to quickly set up a Blogger and a WordPress blog.

Blogger

a. First thing you have to do when setting up Blogger is to sign up for a Google account if you don't already have one. Once you do this you can choose the option "New Blog".

b. Next you fill in your blog name and your desired blog address.

c. Then choose a template from the options on your screen or choose from a more extensive selection when you customize your blog later. After you pick out a template, click the orange "Create Blog!" button.

d. Click the "Start blogging!" link and you'll be brought to a page where you'll create your first post. When you're done click "Publish". Your blog is now live and active.

WordPress

a. When you first get on WordPress's main page, look for the "get Started" link then click it.

b. Fill out the online form with your email, username, password, and blog web address.

c. Once you have chosen an available web name it's time to "Create Blog!"

d. A confirmation email with an embedded link will arrive in your inbox. Clink on the link and you'll be directed to a WordPress page where you would sign in with your username and password.

e. Next you would choose your template and customize your settings and blog appearance.

f. After you've done all that, it's time to create a "New Post". Click "Publish" when you're ready and your blog will be live.

3) During the set up process of your blog, you want to make sure you choose a theme that'll work cohesively with your blog's content. You only get to make one first impression to your visitors and the way your site looks can greatly affect that first impression. The majority of themes are free, but if you'd like to start enhancing your brand and individuality then consider purchasing a custom theme.

4) Install any and all plug-ins, widgets, and other tools that'll make your blog more manageable and visible to search engines. Some popular tools that many people use are:

· Yoast WordPress SEO

- Google XML Sitemaps

- W3 Total Cache

- After the Deadline

- Google Analytics

- All in one SEO pack

- Akismet

5) Start blogging. You can make your first post an introduction to who you are and what this blogs about and what to expect in future posts. Keep your content unique and never duplicate existing content. Not only does it not benefit you, but you can actually get penalized by search engines such as Google for copying another's site content.

Generating Laser Targeted Traffic from your blog

One important factor to having a successful and profitable blog would have to be generating consistent and targeted traffic. This means getting people to actually see, visit and engage in your blog. Without an active audience, your blog will just become stagnant and your chances for making money will slowly disintegrate.

There are many proven ways to generate traffic to your blog. Here are some things you can do to instantly gain traffic.

1) Article Marketing: Writing articles for authority article directories and linking back to your site can help increase exposure for your blog. It can also help to establish your credibility and reputation as a writer or expert in a specific market, niche or topic. If the information you provide is helpful, interesting and relevant then people who read your articles are more inclined to visit your site. You can work exclusively with one directory or diversify your efforts and submit your articles to a couple. Below are some well-known article directories that many people have used to generate traffic for their blogs and other websites.

· eHow

· Squidoo

· Ezine Articles

· Hubpages

· Examiner

· Seeking Alpha

· Technorati

· Article Base

· Buzzle

- GoArticles

- Article99

- ArticleDashBoard

- Valuable Content

2) Guest Posting: If you're comfortable enough to start writing on other people's blog then guest posting is another way you can expand your audience reach. This is especially effective when you guest post for blogs that get pretty good traffic, have a ton of subscribers and consists of numerous back links and if the blog is relevant to your own blog's subject matter.

3) Q & A: Sites People are constantly browsing the web, asking questions, and seeking answers. If you know a thing or two about anything at all then consider answering people's questions on various Q&A websites. The more questions you answer, the more of an expert status you'll have. This will not only build up your credibility, but it'll also incline those whose questions you've answered to come and check out more of your references, including your blog.

Check out some of these popular Q&A sites that you can start answering questions on.

- Yahoo Answers

- Quora

- Answers.com

- Stack Exchange

- Formspring

- AOL Answers

- Web Answers

- All Experts

- Fluther

- Fixya

- Askville

- Mahalo Answers

4) Social Media: Social media networks such as Facebook, Twitter, and LinkedIn are great for getting tons of traffic to your blog. When it comes to using resources like these to generate traffic, it's all about building relationships, expanding your network, and always providing new, up to date and interesting content your friends, followers and subscribers will be excited to check out. Frequently create new content and then post a link back to your blog on your status updates, message boards, tweets, and the like. And if you provide something absolutely too good not too share then you can count on other people to promote and spread the word about your blog. This is how things can go viral and exposure can increase to exponentials amounts. Other social media sites include:

- Pinterest

- MySpace

- Google Plus+

- DeviantArt

- LiveJournal

- Tagged

- Orkut

- CafeMom

· Ning

· Meetup

· myLife

· Multiply

5) Forums: Find heavily populated forums that revolve around your niche or market and become a part of those forums. You never want to go into discussions and threads with a promotional attitude and bombard everyone with links that lead back to your sites and offers. Doing so can get you banned from many forums. It's all about making highly informative and valuable contributions to the community.

Share tips, answers questions, give insight on subjects you're familiar with, or shed light and provide powerful arguments on debatable issues. Once you've joined a forum, the first thing you want to do is creating a signature that's eye catching, interesting, informative, and includes a link back to your blog. Some forums don't allow links in signatures so make sure you join one that does allow it. If people like what you're contributing to the discussions then they'll want to know more about you by clicking on your profile as well as the link in your signature.

6) Blog Commenting: This can be a tedious and very time consuming task, but it's still a great way to generate traffic to your blog. Visit other blogs and leave comments in the comment sections with a link back to your site. Bloggers and sometimes even their visitors will be curious to visit your blog if you leave a comment that's funny, informative or thought provoking that's relevant to the author's post.

7) Interviews: There will come a point when your popularity will begin to grow and other bloggers or websites will want to interview you. This is a great opportunity for more exposure and if the people who are coordinating the interview have websites that are high authority and get a good amount of traffic then you can expect some, if not all, of that traffic to trickle on over to your blog as well.

8) SEO (Search Engine Optimize): Let your content do as much traffic generation as you're doing by applying SEO. SEO will help make your website more visible to search engines such as Google or Yahoo. If you provide unique, quality content then these search engines will reward you with higher page ranking. Anyone who lands on page one or two of any search engine is sure to get a ton of traffic thrown their way with millions of people always searching and browsing the internet for various subjects and topics; one of which could lead them straight to your blog. The last thing we mentioned in regards to traffic generation is applying SEO techniques. This has proven to be very effective over many years when people started to realize how important it was to get on that first page of a search engine.

Step 3: Write eBooks for quick cash

The Ebook Revolution

This chapter tells you why it's time to jump aboard the eBook bandwagon, and where the market's going – but first, here's a thought-provoking quote: "You cannot change anything in your life with intention alone, which can become a watered-down, occasional hope that you'll get to tomorrow. Intention without action is useless" (Caroline Myss, Author of Entering The Castle)

Today is the best time in history for ordinary folk like you and me to become financially independent through eBook publishing. Here's why: People of all ages tend to move with the times and keep pace with technology – even in the darkest corners of Third World Countries. As a result, each day that goes by, more and more folks are swinging away from expensive print books, and embracing the convenience, features, and yes, even the status, of reading eBooks. To add impetus to the snowballing trend, there are untold millions of Kindles, iPads, Sony eReaders and Nooks out there, not to mention the billions of smart phones, tablets, and PC's with preloaded eBook apps. Don't forget escalating hardware sales. For example:

a) Amazon's all-time top selling product, the Kindle eReader, is flying off the shelves so fast, they're struggling to keep up with demand.

b) The sales graphs of Mobile devices look like someone drew a vertical hockey stick on the graph instead of representing reality.

Here's the cherry on top of the cake:

There is a tremendous shortage of eBooks.

For example, Amazon.com, the world's largest book retailer, carries over 26.8 million printed books, and as of mid- 2012, they had less than 800 thousand electronic eBooks to offer...

…and for the first time in publication history, eBooks are outselling print books.

Wow!

Do the math: Shortage + growing demand = the independent publisher's dream. If this isn't the most electrifying opportunity of the century, then I don't know what is…

What's more, the traditional gatekeepers guarding the publishing industry are a rapidly dying breed – The eBook revolution has drained the moat, lowered the drawbridge, and flung the gates of the citadel open. For the first time in history, Independent authors (AKA "Indie" authors) can publish their eBook in a matter of weeks and start earning up to 70 percent royalties.
- No expenses
- No rejection slips
- No agents
- No waiting a year or so for publication
- No more paltry 3 to 5 percent royalties

SO DO IT!

Fill the gap. Give people what they want

– How-To's for instruction, and Fiction for entertainment.

It may take luck and talent to publish successful fiction – but hey, there are millions and millions of bestsellers out there on the Public Domain just waiting for you…

Apart from that, anyone who can tap a keyboard can put an instructional book together with a little help – and that's what we're here for. Before we get started, here are three golden rules to live by:

1. Stick to the basics.
2. Keep it simple.
3. Don't go off at a tangent trying to reinvent the wheel.

Generating Creating eBook Ideas

"We live in a universe of unlimited wealth, because we live in a universe of unlimited ideas. Wealth is nothing more than an idea with action."
(Bob Proctor)

This section explores ways of generating an endless stream of ideas for your next eBook.

A good way to start is to build a list by analyzing your own personal problems, needs, and desires.

- What answers do you search for on the Internet?
- What challenges are you faced with?
- Do you enjoy a particular sport or pastime?
- What are you good at?
- What keeps you awake at night?
- Which subjects fascinate you?
- What makes you laugh, what makes you cry, and what are your pet peeves?

Take a yellow pad and jot everything down, then ask your friends and family the same questions.

Change your mindset

Start thinking "solutions" rather than "problems." In life, each challenge, puzzle, threat, or question, is an opportunity in disguise. Once you use this approach, you'll find fresh new opportunities everywhere. ... Even in the Bible!

I've read the Good Book from cover-to-cover, and one of the of the things that stood out, is that most, if not *all* self-improvement principles, phrases, and ideas used by self-help gurus, actually originate there. To name a few: *Ask and you will receive; Seek and you will find; knock and the door will be opened for you.*

All of these are so very true… Carry a pencil and notebook and think "how-to." Jot down ideas as they occur to you – human memory is notoriously fickle. Like dreams, new ideas and sudden "Aha" moments tend to fade without a written reminder. Speaking of dreams, keep a pad and pencil on your nightstand… It'll take a while to develop your startup list, but you'll be amazed at how big it will grow, but before you start, here's another tip:

Type the words "how to" - "how to learn"- "how to acquire" - "how to win" and "how to teach" into each of the Google, Yahoo!, and Bing search boxes. In every case, these marvelous search engines will immediately flood the search results pages with ten or more of the most sought after solutions people are searching for.

Grab one or two of those subjects and start thinking about your first best seller. Bingo! You now have a nice juicy list of subjects to get your teeth into, and it's time to start refining. Go through the list. Discard the rubbish and wild ideas, and then highlight anything and everything that you're familiar with, good at, and stuff you're interested in.

If you know a lot about a particular subject, you'll be loaded with enthusiasm and eager to start. What's more, you'll understand the buzzwords, so you'll be able to talk directly to your targeted audience – and those people are ready, willing, and able to pay handsomely for information. For example, if you favorite sport happens to be archery, you'll know what "nocking point" and "bracing height" mean without having to resort to Wikipedia – and when you write your eBook, your knowledge, passion, and enthusiasm will shine through like a beacon.

Be careful here. Don't place too much emphasis on your own personal list, because stuff that *you* like doesn't necessarily matter. It's what the *paying public* wants that brings home the bacon. As I said, concentrate on subjects and niches that your soon-to-be readers are likely to pay hard cash for. Especially if answers to their needs and wants are scanty or covered by obvious Get Rich Quick scams.

While we're on the subject, beware of glittering GRQ offers; they're written by some of the worlds' most talented and compelling copywriters – and if you don't have a filtering device between your brain and your credit card, you're sunk…

Regardless of how logical and believable their sales pitches sound, they never work because there's no such thing as a free lunch. According to the laws of physics, man cannot create or destroy energy – and the flip side of *that* cute little law, is that man cannot conjure instantaneous wealth out of thin air without first putting in some serious sweat-equity.

Researching for your first eBook

This chapter covers the importance of content research prior to putting your book together. An eBook containing relevant and accurate information helps to brand your name by building authority, generating reader trust, and acquiring a list of followers. However, the most important benefit comes from positive reviews – and once you get those, your sales will begin to skyrocket.

Research, research, research – even if you think you know your chosen subject backwards. The good news is that since you had the foresight to bookmark relevant pages for later reference, and taken full advantage of Google Trends, you've already covered a lot of ground.

Apart from that, you can easily get to the heart of any subject under the sun by using the search engines intelligently; here's the best way to do that. Remember those fancy search strings we gave you for researching EzineArticles and blogs? All the tricks and techniques we used, together with a lot of other useful stuff, are available online.

Here's a short list of related websites you may want to visit:

http://www.google.com/insidesearch/
http://support.google.com/websearch/bin/hl=en&answer=136861
http://www.slideshare.net/chaumanduc/googlesearch-techniques-1240734
http://blog.simplek12.com/education/7-google-search-techniques/
http://www.lunarforums.com/lunar_chit_chat/html

(This is just the tip of the iceberg; there are many more reference sites out there).

Set up a new "bookmarks" or "favorites" folder, and bookmark the above URL's for quick reference. Practice by using the techniques described as often as possible; you'll soon become fluent in "Google-Speak," and once that happens, you'll be able to zero in and find precisely what you're looking for without having to wade through dozens of pages. Reminder: After locating useful info, choose the relevant research folder and bookmark the page as described earlier.

Structuring your eBook

If you're writing an instructional book, lay out your chapters in logical sequence, and then answer the questions Who? What? When? Where? How? and Why?

For example:

Chapter 1: Introduction.
Chapter 2: Who reads eBooks?
Chapter 3: What are some of the advantages of eBooks?
Chapter 4: When is the best time to publish?
Chapter 5: Where can I find the best free eBooks?
Chapter 6: How do I write, publish, and market eBooks?
Chapter 7: Why should I consider becoming an Indie author?
Chapter 8: Summary of the above information.

This is an over-simplified example. In practice, your book will probably need more than eight chapters. If so, make sure you provide replies to all six questions (in any order) throughout the ensuing chapters.

In other words, include every point needed to convey the information fully and clearly in plain English. If you're writing fiction, prepare a timeline together with a logical sequence of events leading to the climax, and then block out the chapters in the right order. Write each chapter heading. Once that is done, select the MS "Word "Home" tab, highlight the chapter description with your mouse, and click on the "Heading 1" tab in to box on the upper right of the MS Word "Home" window. This will allow you to use the "Table of Contents" feature to insert an automatically linked TOC as described in "Building Your Book for Kindle" and covered in the "Before you Write" section.

TIP

Select the gray "References" tab at the top of the MS Word window and select the leftmost "Table of Contents" tab. Scroll down past the built-in Table of Contents descriptions and click on the "Insert Table of Contents" tab near the bottom. Uncheck the "Show Page Numbers" box and select "1" in the "Show Levels" drop-down menu at the bottom of the window. Press the OK button to build your linked table of contents automatically. After the table appears, press and hold "Ctrl" on your keyboard, point the mouse cursor to the chapter you want to go to, and left click your mouse.

NOTE: The Table of Contents (TOC) is not written in stone. If you add extra chapters or move chapters around during editing, simply delete the original TOC, ensure that all your chapter headings are formatted as "Heading 1," and then build a new TOC. If a pop-up window appears asking. "Do you want to replace the selected Table of Contents?" Click on the "No" button.

Writing your eBook

Take a deep breath, relax, and start writing – it's easier than you think! Forget everything you learned in high school or college English; just apply the K.I.S.S principle (Keep it simple, stupid) while developing your work. Don't use fancy words unless they're absolutely necessary. You're not out to impress readers; you're out to make it as easy as possible for them to absorb information without groping for a dictionary every five minutes.

Avoid writing in the "passive" voice. Open paragraphs and sentences with an active verb, such as: "do, write, insert, open, follow, act, run, jump," and so on. For example, "Here's where you insert the keyword," (passive). "Insert the keyword here," (active). Another example, "If you see a Grizzly bear on the trail, run as fast as you can," (passive). Run as fast as you can if you see a Grizzly bear on the trail," (active). Follow this rule, but don't worry too much, you'll get your knuckles rapped by the Word grammar checker when you slip up; just ignore the advice if it suits your writing style or context related to that particular passage or sentence ;-) Write as you speak, not as the English teachers want you to write. Pretend that you're speaking directly to your closest friend. Visualize his or her face as you write. Go ahead. Dangle participles, split infinitives, end sentences with a preposition if necessary, and use slang and buzzwords sparingly – never formalize your work by sticking rigidly to the principles taught in high school. The words flow, and hopefully, the reader get the point – and that's what counts.

Structure your chapters this way:

1 - Tell them what you're going to tell them.
2 - Tell them.
3 – Then tell them what you told them in a summary chapter at the end of the book, or at the end of each major section.

Copy and paste your researched material directly from the website into the top of the page you're working on, and then rewrite everything underneath, using your own words and personal slant. Mix it up. Try not to duplicate the same points-sequence used in the original, and use synonyms wherever appropriate. Just highlight the word, right click, and choose "Synonyms" from the drop-down menu. Use short sentences. Do not duplicate important words in the same passage or repeat yourself elsewhere in the book. If you do so intentionally, offer an "as mentioned above" type remark; your readers are smarter than you think. Check your spelling regularly and be alert for out of context words, such as "your" instead of "you're." Inspect your work for repeats of your favorite expressions and buzzwords. Don't ramble – and AVOID CLICHES (sorry for shouting).

For instructional books, break the material down into small, bite-sized chunks, and try to limit paragraph length to between one and four sentences; however, avoid monotony by inserting a longer paragraph every now and then. As mentioned earlier, when you're satisfied, copy and paste the material chapter-by-chapter onto a plagiarism checker such as "Search Engine Reports" or "Copyscape." Rewrite as necessary if the software flags your material as plagiarism – when that's done, no one will cry "foul," as long as you use your own words and stick to rules of "Fair Use Provision."

Your eBook Cover

Your cover is the first thing a prospective buyer sees when surfing the vendor's bookshelf. This chapter explains how to attract attention with eye-catching graphics. Your first option is to do it yourself using "MS Paint" or similar. This presentation walks you through all the steps one at a time. If you happen to be a proficient Photoshop artist and own the software, you can use that instead of MS Paint. Here's the URL:

http://www.youtube.com/watch?v=0H0k_BFcD04.

Follow the steps, but create a flat image sized at the latest Kindle requirements; at the time of writing, they stood at 1000 pixels high and 676 pixels wide. Use vibrant and contrasting colors, and use free or paid images if applicable. Finally, save the image in .jpg format. BTW, all photographs and images used in Wikipedia are in the public domain, and there are plenty of free stock photos available on the Internet. However, if push comes to shove, download a suitable paid image from one of the image libraries, such as "dreamstime.com."

The second alternative is to go to www,fiverr.com and type "eBook cover" into the search box; you'll find a long list if graphic artist willing to produce an eye-catching cover for the princely sum of $5. At that price, you can always commission two or three different artists and then choose the most appropriate illustration. Spread it around, and don't commission the same artist to produce multiple examples.

Your third alternative is to find a graphics professional on the Internet specializing in eBook covers; this works best in the long run, but it's the most expensive option. However, if you're working on a tight budget, you can always start with one of the first two options and then upload a professionally crafted cover later.

Front Pages and Editing

The first thing to do is to center your title and author's name on the first page of your manuscript followed by a page break. Then use the next page to block out your copyright. You don't have to get all fancy with flowery legalese; there are only two elements required:

1) A copyright notice with the copyright symbol included, such as "© 2012 Jane Doe."
2) A declaration stating that the rights to reproduce the work are reserved by the copyright holder (click on the following URL for more info).
http://www.theBookdesigner.com/2010/01/samples-you-can-copy-and-pasteinto- your-book/ for more info).

The above website allows you to change the details and simply copy and paste the following example into your copyright page:

Copyright © 2012 by Wile E. Coyote

All rights reserved. This book or any portion thereof may not be reproduced or used in any manner whatsoever without the express written permission of the publisher, except for the use of brief quotations in a book review. Produced in the United States of America First edition, 2012 ISBN 0-9000000-0-0 Falling Anvil Publishing 123 Mesa Street Scottsdale, AZ 00000 www.FallingAnvilBooks.com (your website URL goes here).

Note: the ISBN is only required if you plan to distribute your eBook or print version through multiple outlets. If marketed solely via Amazon Kindle, insert the assigned ASIN (Amazon Standard Item Number) instead.

Publishing Your Book on Kindle Marketplace

To get the ball rolling, publish your book on Kindle before going elsewhere. You get the widest coverage and the maximum number of sales there. Before you begin, download the free eBook, *Publish on Amazon with Kindle Direct Publishing.* Here's the URL: http://www.amazon.com/Publish-   Amazon-Kindle-Publishingebook/dp/B004LX069M/ref=sr_1_2?s=books&ie=UTF8 &qid=1347970417&sr=2&keywords=Publish+on+Amazon+with+

Read this book carefully; it will guide you through all the publishing steps and broaden your knowledge base.

Ensure that your MS Word .doc manuscript is properly formatted. Even though you may have been very careful when writing the book, quirky little formatting errors inevitably infiltrate the text during rewrites and editing – and these seemingly insignificant additions sometimes scramble text alignment and paragraph spacing during the HTML conversion process.

Although it takes an hour or two, the safest way to have a perfectly "clean" manuscript is to carry out a full reformatting exercise as follows:

1. Press the "Select" arrow on the extreme right of the MS Word "Home" panel. Press the "select all" option to highlight the entire manuscript and then copy and paste the manuscript into a plain text notepad.

2. Once you've done that, reverse the process. Copy and paste the plain text back into a blank MS Word page.

3. Highlight the entire document and carry out the paragraph formatting procedure as described in the "Before you Write" chapter, and don't forget to indent the first line by .01 if you're using block paragraphs separated by a space.

4. Scan through the document and correct any paragraph spacing errors that appear, by either adding or deleting spaces between paragraphs.

5. Insert Page breaks at the foot of each of your front pages, and at the end of each chapter throughout the book. While you're doing this, highlight each chapter headline and press the "Heading 1" button on the MS Word "Home" page.

6. Delete the original Table of Contents and build a new one, and don't forget to add a page break after the TOC.

7. Reinstate all bold, underlined, or italic formatting carried out in the original manuscript, and save the manuscript in "Word 97 – 2003 document" format.

Convert you manuscript into HTML format as follows:

With the document open, hit the "save as" button and select your desktop as the destination. Click on the "Save as Type" drop down menu, then select "Web Page, Filtered" option and save the file to your desktop. Go to Kindle Direct Publishing www.kdp.amazon.com and sign in or register for an Amazon self-publishing account. The program then takes you to the KDP Admin panel labeled "Bookshelf." Click on the "Add New Title" button. The program then opens up a series of forms and walks you through the steps, including how to list the book's title and description, and how to upload your cover graphics. They also provide "read more" buttons to explain the finer points. After uploading your manuscript, look a little further down the page and click on the small blue notification that says "download book previewer file." Go back to your computer; you'll see your book as it appears on a regular Kindle eReader. Run another editing and proofreading exercise – you'll be amazed how overlooked errors jump off the page...

Save the file after taking care of the necessary amendments. Repeat the "Upload your Book File exercise and click on the "Save and Publish" button. After vetting the manuscript, Amazon assigns a unique ASIN number to the work, and approximately 12 hours later, your masterpiece appears on Kindle's virtual bookshelf.

TIP

Study the "Getting the Most out of Amazon Kindle" chapter in "Book Three," and incorporate those ideas while going through the upload process. – Consider signing up for "KDP Select" for the first 90-day period. Once the money starts rolling in, and after the 90-day KDP select launch, have the book professionally formatted for other eReaders, and then list your blockbuster on Barnes and Noble, Apple, and Kobe.

Don't worry; the submission process is similar to the KDP steps outlined above. However, having said all that, take my advice and re-publish your eBook through Smashwords. This publisher does it all for you. They format your manuscript in all the known eBook formats, and they submit your work to Apple, Barnes and Noble, Kobe, and all the other major retailers around the world. Here's the URL:

http://www.smashwords.com/.

They also give you an ISBN number (required by Apple and B&N), and they take care of a bunch of other stuff to help boost your sales – and they do it all for a small percentage of your royalties.

Publishing your book on the ClickBank Marketplace

ClickBank is a multi-faceted organization offering three ways to leverage eBook income as follows:

1 - Use the "find" feature in the ClickBank marketplace to chase down profitable eBook titles.

2 - Market your own digital book directly, and leverage sales by attracting a team of motivated affiliate marketers willing to sell your product on commission.

3 - Become a ClickBank affiliate and develop an extra stream of income through affiliate commission.

Before eReaders hit the marketplace, Clickbank had many thousands of titles available for instant PDF download. In fact, even now, they probably offer more instructional book titles than Amazon does. Log onto https://www.clickbank.com/index.html and click the "Marketplace" tab at the top of the page. Enter your keyword in the search box to get a list of related books.

Drill down and look for "Grav" numbers exceeding 10; gravity tells you how much action the book is getting. (BTW, don't forget to list interesting ideas into your main spreadsheet under "ClickBank Gravity").

Now, click on the title of the first book that looks promising. This takes you to the landing page. Read the sales copy to find out if it's credible and well written, and then ask yourself if you'd be tempted to click on the "Buy" button. If so, download the book and study it. After that, ask yourself if there are any important points, answers, or benefits the author missed. Then ask yourself if you could improve on the book by finding a new angle and/or by offering added value.

If that's the case, fire up a competitive book in the same genre, add an eye catching cover, and have at it! Do what Tony Waters did and market carefully selected digital books through ClickBank. This will enable you to sell your work for up to 10 times more than dedicated eBook vendors are willing pay, and you won't need to format it for eReaders.

Follow the steps outlined in "How to Create an EBook," but instead of formatting it for eReaders, convert your Word document to PDF format. If the MS word "save as PDF" function disappoints you, either use one of the many PDF converters available online, or take advantage of the free facility offered by the "Free PDF Converter" website. Prepare your cover graphics, but include a 3D image instead of the flat cover called for by Amazon and other eBook vendors.

Set up a one-page blog. List your eBook title as the domain name, and then create a landing page. Just follow the advice listed in the "How to Sell" section and prepare an effective enthusiastic sales letter with an illustration of the 3D cover. Study other vendors' landing pages on ClickBank for ideas regarding layout and color schemes. Finish with a powerful call to action and include a "Buy Now" button linked to the ClickBank checkout page.

ClickBank offers a unique online retail environment for digital products. In addition, they have more than 100,000 active affiliate marketers eager to promote your product in exchange for a commission. Use the Clickbank team of consultants. They'll help you settle on a realistic retail price, and they'll also advise you on how much affiliate commission to offer. After settling on the financial details, submit your book for approval. Once your product is approved, pay the onetime $49.95 activation fee. Your book goes live on the ClickBank Marketplace within an hour or so, and it becomes available for affiliates to promote – and you're in business! ClickBank pays you and your affiliates automatically for each confirmed sale, either by direct bank transfer or by check.

Open a ClickBank account if you haven't already done so. Go to the Marketplace. Find a suitable book as described above, and go to the landing page. If the landing page fails to excite you, but you want to promote the book, build your own landing page using Dan Kennedy's principles. Once that's done, publish it on your website or on a one page blog. Next, click the green "Promote" button. ClickBank then issues you with a unique affiliate hoplink to that particular product, and takes you to the existing landing page. Buy a copy. Study it carefully, and then write a review on your website. Put yourself in the role of Devil's Advocate by posting an impartial report listing the good, bad, and indifferent aspects of the work. Once you've summarized your opinions by subtly stressing benefits, buy a good "Link Cloaker," such as the truly excellent "Ninja" from http://ninjalinkcloaker.com/, and add a cloaked link to the vendor's landing page.

Why cloaked? You may lose credibility if the prospect hovers her mouse pointer over the hyperlink and looks at the bottom left of the page. If she sees a long URL featuring your ClickBank affiliate hoplink, she'll know that you stand to profit by offering a tempting review. As a result, she may bypass the link on principal and rob you of commission by going direct. Using a cloaked link also guards against some unscrupulous person hijacking your link and stealing your hard-earned commission.

Check out http://www.cbtrends.com/. Follow through by studying the titles and trends. Examine the gravity figures; you'll find a whole heap of popular, fast moving books ready for you to emulate, improve upon, and publish with a sparkling new title and an eye-catching cover.

The second site to use is http://www.markosweb.com/www/cbengine.however, they don't dig as deep or go into as much detail as cbtrends. I could go on and on describing different ways to leverage ClickBank income, however, that's beyond the scope of this book. Besides, others have already done it far more effectively than I can, so why re-invent the wheel? Here's a short list of websites offering tips and ideas, some of which will give you goosebumps.

http://www.clickbanksuccessforum.com/forum/
http://www.clickbank.com/blog/
http://www.clickbankguide.com/

Please don't allow these tempting ClickBank opportunities to divert you from your main goal; rather put them on the back burner until you have three or four eBooks up and running on Amazon Kindle, and you've developed a website. Once you've reached that stage, you'll be ready to spread your wings.

Marketing your book

A large percentage of Indie Authors make a good living by simply listing book after book on Kindle, and then relying on Amazon's marketing infrastructure to bring in the business. However, whether they know it or not, those "Kindle-Only" authors leave hundreds, if not thousands of dollars on the table every month, by ignoring online and offline marketing techniques. What's worse, many eBooks never make it to the checkout counter, simply because their authors failed to follow Amazon's (almost) foolproof system.

Having said that, most Kindle eBooks do sell – provided the author does everything possible to mesh their titles seamlessly into Kindle's built-in marketing system – and one if the most efficient ways of doing that, is to position your book squarely in the path of your prospective buyer(s). Imagine what would have happened if the (then) unknown author of *Fifty shades of Grey* simply plonked her book down in the middle of the fiction category without bothering to promote the book, or even list it under the "Adult" sub category. With that unimposing cover and obscure title, the book could easily have been buried under thousands of other eBooks vying for attention until someone found it by mistake.

Amazon owns the largest, most efficient buyer orientated search engine on earth, and with the right moves, you can take your sales to an entirely new level by using certain options, together with some ridiculously simple Search Engine Optimization (SEO) techniques, and a few on-page and off-page procedures. Once buyers notice a tempting title with a couple of five-star ratings, impulse buying takes over and the sale is virtually guaranteed. What's more, impulse buying is further augmented by Amazon having over *two hundred million credit cards* on file.

Consequently purchasing books on Amazon's "no-hassle one-click ordering system," is ridiculously easy... The following chapters explain how to get the best results from Kindle's marketing system, as well as the most effective ways of multiplying sales through various online and offline marketing methods.

Step 4: Monetizing YouTube Channel

If you have a YouTube channel and you like uploading videos, you can turn your hobby into a money making opportunity.

First, you have to add keywords so other people can find your channel. You can navigate to the Advanced section of the Channel settings to include your preferred keywords. See to it that the keywords you choose are relevant to what you upload on your channel.

Also, you may want to consider changing your username if it is not related to your channel or if it is difficult to remember and pronounce. As much as possible, you should use a username that will stick to the memory of your viewers. Keep it short but catchy. Refrain from using symbols or characters that will make it difficult for your viewers to type in the search box.

Next, you have to add the content. If you have a high quality camera, use it. If you don't, you can use your cellphone as long as the video is clear. High quality videos are preferred by viewers though. Also, you should not make them bored by uploading really long videos.

You have to upload regularly to keep your subscribers interested and entertained. You also have to be consistent with your uploads. Otherwise, your viewers will be disappointed because they expect a certain type of video to be uploaded. If you do not give them what they want to see, the will unsubscribe from your channel. Do not forget to tag your videos and write good descriptions.

You can embed your YouTube channel in your blog or website to gain more viewers. You can also paste links to it in your social networking accounts. The more people know about your channel, the more views you will have.

Finally, there is the monetization part. In order to make money off your videos, you have to enable the monetization feature. This allows ads to pop up in your videos. Monetizing your videos also makes you agree that you cannot upload copyrighted material on your channel.

You can also set up Google Adsense. Just go to their website and sign up to create an account. The rules say that you have to be at least eighteen years old to sign up. You need a bank account or a PayPal account, as well as a mailing address to receive the payments. You get to earn money each time someone clicks on the ads on your videos.

Step 5: Make money using Shutterstock

Did you know that you could earn money for being creative? Shutterstock allows you to submit images and videos while giving you royalties for every sale made. Today, most of us have a DSLR camera. All you need is some knowledge of photography and videography and you are good to go.

Shutterstock offers a marketplace to help you earn money on autopilot. The site boasts of more than 35 million royalty-free images and 1.7 million footage clips. They served more than 400 million downloads to nearly 1 million customers in over 150 countries.

In fact, the website is a leading source of revenue for photographers, illustrators, and videographers.

So, let us come to the next question.

What are stock images?

Simply put, stock images refers to any art that exists and is ready for reuse. Shutterstock maintains a library of such reusable images subject to different licenses for usage. People often relate 'stock' with imagery but it consist of videos and illustrations as well. What's more exciting is that stock imagery has grown into a multi-billion-dollar industry.

What to create

Images speak volumes where words fail. So where do you find inspiration for your stock imagery?

Start with a paper notebook, a tablet computer, a smartphone, or a desktop. Here are some places to get ideas for the imagery you create.

1. **Social Media and Online Tools**: Look at trending topics, influential people in news, issues or controversies, etc.

2. **The Newsstand**. Scan the latest headlines and look for common themes. Are there any political issues making headlines due to election? What topics are trending? Is there a new chic trend or style in the market in homes and gardening section?

3. **Fashion and home furnishing:** look for the most popular color. What are the emerging looks in this year's fashion show? What are the styles used in home and garden magazines?

4. Technology: Look at the latest technology blogs like mashable. What type of products and technology make headlines? What products are displayed – cellphones, tablets, computers, etc. What is the changing trend?

5. Calendar: What are the most prominent cultural, social, and news events. What is happening locally? What's happening at the local food, fashion, religion, cultural, architectural fronts? Look for holidays and celebrations to get ideas.

6. Contemporary art: Never copy someone else's work but it can surely give you inspiration to the world of art. Look for new techniques. Look for what's trending in the market.

What Buyers Are Begging For

To bolster your objective of earning money on Shutterstock, you need to understand what your buyers are looking for. They are always on a prowl of images that show authenticity. Perfectly posed images with beautiful models are popular. They want it to be inspirational, professional, 'real', relaxed, and natural. Something that shows creativity. Different buyers have different expectations. Some may say your image is creative but the model in it is not smiling. Or the background color is not too bright. Think about a newspaper or a magazine cover. What do you need to make it appealing to everyone? Think from that perspective and the rest will flow. Popular themes include nature, objects, business, and healthcare if you are beginner.

How to Maximize Your Profits When Shooting

Here are top tips to maximize your earning potential.

1. Rent, do not buy: Always get equipment on rent as storage, maintenance, etc. can be quite expensive. Moreover, the technology you have invested in today will be obsolete tomorrow. These equipment are expensive and renting it makes perfect sense.

2. Sharing is caring: If you know of other photographs, ask them about sharing production costs.

3. Shoot multiple scenes with your models: This is the most important tip. People are looking for portfolios of models doing different things – different sets, angles, facial expressions, clothing, scenarios, orientations, etc. maximize your returns.

Shoot video and stills at the same time. Most cameras have a HD capability and can capture lovely videos.

4. Shoot videos to get much higher royalties. Royalties at Shutterstock are as high as $23 per download.

5. Keywording: Shooting an amazing image is good but it is useless if no one can locate it. To sell your photos, you need to add accurate keywords. Think like a buyer. What is the person likely to search to download your image? Determine 25-45 accurate keywords and customize them for every image. As a rule of thumb, put 25-45 keyword per image.

Making Money at Shutterstock

Technically, buyers do not 'buy' your images. Rather, they license them. You still own the rights to distribute and display your images and video, but a license gives the buyer permission to use your photos. Each time someone buys a license, you get a royalty fee.

You can see each of the license types and their associated royalty amounts on our earnings schedule:
http://submit.shutterstock.com/earnings_schedule.mhtml

Step 6: Welcome to the world of affiliate marketing

You have learned about affiliate marketing from the previous chapters. You can incorporate it into blogging, website building, and even on your YouTube channel. As long as you collaborate with an online merchant and receive a payment for every referral, sale, or ad clicked, you are into affiliate marketing.

Anyway, if you want to be a successful affiliate marketer, you should get rid of the following thoughts and beliefs:

- Affiliate systems are easy and quick to manage.

Affiliate marketing program takes a lot of work. In most situations, you may even be faced with a lot of competition. This only means that you cannot get rich quickly. Entrepreneurs and business owners assume that all you have to do is set up a website and select an affiliate to associate with. They think that you can simply let things run their course.

However, according to statistics from Three Ladders Marketing, just 0.6% of affiliate marketers are still in the industry since 2013. This means that the rest have given up. Affiliate marketing may earn you a passive income, but you will not be able to succeed in it without devoting a significant amount of time and effort.

Keep in mind that affiliate marketing basically relies on building relationships. Such relationships can be fostered by searching for more efficient and better partnerships, bring the right partner into your program, and regularly updating your content to keep things fresh and new.

The affiliate program will help bring traffic to your site, but it is still up to you to turn that traffic into conversions.

- You have to work in a lucrative and highly popular nice to succeed in affiliate marketing.

Sadly, many companies do not bother to try affiliate marketing programs because they do not think that their market is big enough. Some of them even try to go into bigger niches. While it is true that high-profiled niches do well with affiliate marketing, this does not mean that you cannot succeed if you do not go with such niches. You can still succeed if you abide by the mission statement of the company and stick with affiliates who know the importance of working in a comfortable market.

- Affiliate marketing is no longer as effective as before.

Due to the new algorithms of Google, link building has become less and less popular. Because of this affiliate marketers have become discouraged to continue this venture. However, you should realize that there are still a lot of ways on how you can use search engine optimization to build your brand.

What are the Best Affiliate Programs?

From the Affiliate Blogging chapter, you have read about the best affiliate programs for bloggers. If you are a beginner, however, you can benefit the most from the following affiliate programs:

ClickBank

It offers unique features that make it excellent for beginners. For instance, you can sign up without having to own an established website. You also get to access educational and service support. What makes it different from the others is that it distributes its own products instead of using a middleman. So, you will be dealing with the supplier directly instead of relying on multiple agencies to provide the services.

Amazon Associates

It has its own warehouse and also distributes its own products. In addition, it has a massive collection of products that you can promote. Amazon also offers an easy to use toolbox for creating ads, including customizable widgets. What's more, it has a support forum wherein you can interact with other affiliates.

Commission Junction

It is one of the oldest affiliate marketing companies. However, it only offers an advertising platform. It does not distributes products or offer customer service. Hence, you have to directly contact the companies that you promote.

LinkShare

Just like Commission Junction, it does not distribute products. Nevertheless, it is still ideal for beginners because it has a simple interface. It also offers QuickTour, which guides beginners.

ShareASale

It is another middle-man style affiliate program that does not distribute products. It is known to be people-oriented and not so much number-oriented. It also hosts an internal social network for affiliates and merchants to interact with each other.

Step 7: Generate your passive income through informational products

What does it mean when you offer an informational e-course product? Well, it means that you sell your knowledge about certain subjects through PDFs, eBooks, webinars, and live speaking engagements among other platforms. If you want to be successful in this venture, you have to keep the following pointers in mind:

- **Be serious about it.**

You have to stay focused and motivated for at least twelve months. You may experience some failures in the beginning, but this should not be a reason for you to back out and quit.

- **Have an editorial calendar.**

Think of what you want to share to your audience. This could be anything, as long as it is helpful, interesting, and informative. You can share case studies, interviews, hacks, or reviews. Make use of a calendar to help you stay right on track.

- **Promote your blog posts.**

You can use various platforms to promote your blog posts. For instance, you can take advantage of social networking sites. You can create a fan page that targets people you know might be interested in the e-course products that you offer. Make sure that your blog posts discuss these e-course products in detail.

- **Collect email addresses with one or two-page PDF's.**

See to it that your PDF's are exclusive and interesting. They can be mini eBooks, checklists, or case studies. Use titles that are catchy and would make your readers curious as to what they contain. Once you are able to collect email addresses, you can send out your blog posts as newsletters. Do not hesitate to ask your readers to leave comments. You can also encourage returning visitors to leave their email addresses on your website so they can receive your newsletters.

- **Do guest blog posts and live webinars.**

After several months, you can research about the popular blogs that talk about your subjects. Collaborate with them and do some guest blog posts. This way, you can get more traffic for your blog and improve your credibility. Likewise, you can launch free webinars when you reach your target number of subscribers.

Putting it All Together

I would like to thank you for taking the journey through this book with me. I spent countless hours trying to show you exactly what recipe worked for me, because I want you to be prosperous.

The time has come where I cut you loose and you take this thing to the next level. The key is in your hand, all you have to do is unlock your full potential and consequently a passive revenue stream will be unlocked as well.

I wish you the best of luck and I hope to see you on the web soon!

"Our greatest weakness lies in giving up. The most certain way to succeed is always to try just one more time."
Thomas A. Edison

www.ingramcontent.com/pod-product-compliance
Lightning Source LLC
Chambersburg PA
CBHW071000180526
45168CB00003B/1227